A Special Gift

For:

From:

Date:

Illustration Copyright © 1998 Kristin Wenning
Text Copyright © 1998

Brownlow Publishing Company
6309 Airport Freeway
Fort Worth, Texas 76117

ISBN: 1-57051-251-5

Printed in China

A Little Book of

Brownlow

Love

Compiled by Rhonda S. Hogan • Illustrated by Kristin Wenning

Kris-10

Little Treasures Miniature Books

A Little Cup of Tea

A Little Nest of Pleasant Thoughts

All Things Great & Small

All Things Grow With Love

Angels of Friendship

Baby's First Little Bible

Baby's First Little Book

Baby's First Little Book of Angels

Beside Still Waters • Dear Daughter

Dear Teacher • Faithful Friends

For My Secret Pal

Grandmothers Are for Loving

Mother–The Heart of the Home

My Sister, My Friend

Quiet Moments of Inspiration • Quilted Hearts

Rose Petals • Season of Friendship

Soft As the Voice of an Angel

Tea Time Friends • They Call It Golf

There is no difficulty that
enough love will not conquer...
No door that enough love will not open:

EMMETT FOX

One word frees us of all the weight
and pain of life: That word is love.

SOPHOCLES

Dear friends,
let us love
one another,
for love comes
from God.

1 JOHN 4:7

Love cannot be forced,
love cannot be
coaxed and teased.
It comes out of Heaven
unasked and unsought.

PEARL BUCK

We cannot

really love anybody

with whom we

never laugh.

AGNES REPPLIER

When you know that God loves you, it
helps you love yourself.
And when you love yourself, you
can love somebody else.

KARL MILTON

When love reigns,

the impossible may be attained.

INDIAN PROVERB

Those who are habitually
performing small acts of kindness
do the great acts of love.

RHONDA S. HOGAN

There are more people
who wish to be loved than there
are who are willing to love.

ANONYMOUS

Kris-10

Work is what gives us our bread and butter, stability and place in the world, but love keeps us human. Any old kind of love.

BARBARA HOLLAND

A life without love is like a year without summer.

Love all God's creation, both the whole and every grain of sand. Love every leaf, every ray of light. Love the animals, love the plants, love each separate thing. If you love each thing you will perceive the mystery of God in all; and when once you perceive this, you will from that time on grow every day to a fuller understanding of it until you come at last to love the whole world with a love that will then be all~embracing and universal.

FYODOR DOSTOEVSKY

Kris-10

Live well.

Laugh often.

Love much.

ANONYMOUS

Love is a joy that cannot be seen...

a tie that cannot be broken.

THOMAS MALLOY

We do not love people

because they are beautiful;

they seem beautiful to us

because we love them.

LEW WALLACE

Our Lord does not care so much for

the importance of our works as for

the love with which they are done.

TERESA OF AVILA

Dear children let us not love with words

or tongue but with actions and in truth.

1 JOHN 3:18

Time flies,
Suns rise
And Shadows fall.
Let time go by.
Love is forever over all.

ANONYMOUS

Love is the only thing that we
can carry with us when we go,
and it makes the end so easy.

LOUISA MAY ALCOTT

The earth is filled
with your love, O Lord.

PSALM 119:64

Nothing is sweeter than love,

nothing stronger, nothing higher,

nothing wider, nothing more pleasant,

nothing fuller or better

in heaven or on earth.

THOMAS À KEMPIS

When you love someone, you love the whole person, just as he or she is, and not as you would like them to be.

LEO TOLSTOY

The great tragedy of life is not that men perish, but that they cease to love.

W. SOMERSET MAUGHAM

Do not keep the alabaster box of your love and friendship sealed up until your friends are dead. Fill their lives with sweetness. Speak approving, cheering words while their ears can hear them, and while their hearts can be thrilled and made happier. The kind things you mean to say when they are gone, say before they go.

GEORGE W. CHILDS

Let all that you do

be done in love.

1 Corinthians 16:14

The only power which can resist

the power of fear

is the power of love.

Alan Stewart Paton

Love builds memories

that endure, to be treasured

up as hints of what

shall be hereafter.

F. JARRET

Love doesn't make
the world go round.
Love is what makes
the ride worthwhile.

F. P. JONES

To be with those we love is enough.

Ah, how true it is! And it is a

Happiness which will

outlast this life.

In this thought I love to rest.

MADAME SWETCHINE

Loving, like prayer, is a power

as well as a process.

It's curative. It's creative.

ZONA GALE

Love is the only force capable of

transforming an enemy into a friend.

MARTIN LUTHER KING, JR.

Those who give

love, gather love.

ANONYMOUS

Give all to love;

obey thy heart.

RALPH WALDO EMERSON

You have heard that it was said,
"Love your neighbor and hate your enemy."
But I tell you: Love your enemies and
pray for those who persecute you.

MATTHEW 5:43, 44

Love is the best
thing in the world,
and the thing that
lives longest.

HENRY VAN DYKE

Therefore as God's chosen people,

holy and dearly loved,

clothe yourselves with

compassion, kindness, humility,

gentleness, and patience.

COLOSSIANS 3:12

The love of our neighbor is the only door out of the dungeon of self.

GEORGE MACDONALD

The one thing we can never get enough of is love. And the one thing we never give enough of is love.

HENRY MILLER

It probably would be all right if
we'd love our neighbors as we
love ourselves, but could they
stand that much affection?

ANONYMOUS

Love is not getting, but giving.
It is sacrifice. And sacrifice is glorious.

JOANA FIELD

Do not think that love, in order to be genuine, has to be extraordinary. What we need is to love without getting tired. Be faithful in small things because it is in them that your strength lies.

MOTHER TERESA

Love from one being to another
can only be that two solitudes
come nearer, recognize and protect
and comfort each other.

HAN SUYIN

The heart sees better than the eye.

JEWISH PROVERB

It is in loving, not in being loved,
the heart is blessed;
It is in giving, not in seeking gifts,
we find our quest;
Whatever be your longing or
your need, that give—
So shall your soul be fed,
and you indeed shall live.

ANONYMOUS

Love is but the

discovery of ourselves

in others,

and the delight

in the recognition.

ALEXANDER SMITH

The secret of being
loved is being lovely;
and the secret of
being lovely is
being unselfish.

J. G. HOLLAND

To love is to admire with the heart;

to admire is to love with the mind.

THEOPHILE E. GAUTIER

We are shaped and fashioned

by what we love.

GOETHE

We love because he first loved us.

1 JOHN 4:19

Keep love in your heart. A life without it is like a sunless garden when the flowers are dead. The consciousness of loving and being loved brings a warmth and richness to life that nothing else can bring.

OSCAR WILDE

To love is to receive a glimpse of heaven.

KAREN SUNDE

He who is filled with love,

is filled with God himself.

AUGUSTINE

There is a wealth of unexpressed

love in the world.

ARTHUR HOPKINS

I like not only
to be loved,
but to be told
I am loved.

GEORGE ELIOT (MARY ANNE EVANS)

Love and faithfulness

meet together;

righteousness and peace

kiss each other.

Psalm 85:10

Age does not protect
you from love.
But love to some extent
protects you from age.

JEANNE MOREAU

Love can be understood only "from the inside," as a language can be understood only by someone who speaks it, as a world can be understood only by someone who lives in it.

ROBERT C. SOLOMAN